The Real Deal
TOBACCO

Rachel Lynette

Heinemann Library
Chicago, Illinois

Customer Service 888-454-2279
Visit our website at www.heinemannraintree.com

Designed by Richard Parker and Tinstar Design Ltd, www.tinstar.co.uk
Printed and bound in China by Leo Paper Group

12 11 10 09 08
10 9 8 7 6 5 4 3 2 1

Library of Congress Cataloging-in-Publication Data
Lynette, Rachel.
  Tobacco / Rachel Lynette.
     p. cm.
  Includes bibliographical references and index.
  ISBN 978-1-4034-9696-6 (hardback : alk. paper) -- ISBN 978-1-4034-9703-1 (pbk. : alk. paper)
  1. Tobacco use--Health aspects--Juvenile literature. 2. Smoking--Health aspects--Juvenile literature. 3. Nicotine--Health aspects--Juvenile literature. I. Title.
  RA1242.T6L96 2008
  613.85--dc22
                    2007011176

Acknowledgments
The publishers would like to thank the following for permission to reproduce photographs: Alamy/Aliki Image Library/Kathleen Watmough p. **4**; Bubbles p. **19**; Corbis pp. **12** (Zefa/Alan Schein), **14** (Ramin Talaie), **16** (Bettmann), **17** (James Leynse), **18** (Jerry Arcieri), **21** (Zefa/Michael A. Keller), **23** (Michael Reynolds); Getty Images pp. **5** (Photographer's Choice/Garry Gay), **9** (Stone+/Karen Moskowitz), **13** (AFP/Pedro Armestre); Mediscan p. **11**; Photolibrary.com/Index Stock Imagery/Mike Robinson p. **27**; Rex Features pp. **22** (Ventureli), **24** (Andy Paradise), **25** (Buzz Pictures/Roger Sharp); Science Photo Library pp. **8 left**, **8 right** (James Steveson), **15** (Conor Caffrey), **20**, **26** (Doug Martin); SuperStock/ Kwame Zikomo p. **6**.

Cover photograph of an arrow road sign reproduced with permission of iStockphoto/Nicholas Belton; cover photographs of a lit cigarette in an ashtray and a single unlit cigarette reproduced with permission of Getty Images/PhotoDisc .

Every effort has been made to contact copyright holders of any material reproduced in this book. Any omissions will be rectified in subsequent printings if notice is given to the publishers.

The publishers would like to thank Kate Madden for her help in the preparation of this book.

Disclaimer
All the Internet addresses (URLs) given in this book were valid at the time of going to press. However, due to the dynamic nature of the Internet, some addresses may have changed, or sites may have changed or ceased to exist since publication. While the author and publishers regret any inconvenience this may cause readers, no responsibility for any such changes can be accepted by either the author or the publishers.

Contents

Some words are shown in bold, **like this**. You can find out what they mean by looking in the Glossary.

What Is Tobacco?

Tobacco is a broad-leafed plant that is part of the nightshade family of plants. The tobacco plant contains a substance called **nicotine**. Nicotine is poisonous. A single drop of pure nicotine can kill a person in less than a minute. The small amounts of nicotine in tobacco products are not nearly enough to kill someone right away, but over time nicotine can do serious damage to a person's body.

Nicotine is also **addictive**. When people start using tobacco, the nicotine will make them want to continue to use it. Tobacco users experience strong **cravings** and feel very uncomfortable if they try to stop. Once a person starts using tobacco products, it is very difficult for him or her to quit. Tobacco has been shown to be as addictive as drugs such as **cocaine** and **heroin.**

NEWSFLASH

A study in 2003 found that addiction to nicotine may start the first time a person smokes. Seventh graders who had smoked only one or two cigarettes reported feeling nicotine cravings and other signs of addiction. This study supports the idea that it is very easy to become addicted to nicotine.

Tobacco is made from the dried and shredded leaves of the tobacco plant.

Tobacco comes in several different forms.

How is tobacco used?

Most people use tobacco by smoking the dried, shredded leaves in cigarettes. Dried tobacco can also be smoked in pipes and cigars. Some people smoke tobacco in flavored cigarettes from India called *bidis*, or in Indonesian cigarettes flavored with cloves, called *kreteks*.

Tobacco can also be chewed. People who chew tobacco do not swallow it. They chew it for a while and then spit it out. Chewing tobacco is made by forming leaves into blocks called plugs. Another kind of tobacco that is not smoked is called snuff. Snuff is made by grinding tobacco leaves into a fine powder. Snuff is held inside the mouth and then spat out. Some people inhale snuff through the nose.

The Physical Effects of Smoking

When people smoke, they feel the effects of nicotine almost immediately. It takes less than 10 seconds for nicotine to reach the brain. Nicotine causes the brain to produce chemicals that give the smoker a pleasant feeling. It can also make the smoker feel more alert or more relaxed.

Cigarette smoke goes directly into the lungs when it is inhaled. The smoke irritates the throat and the lungs. This can cause the smoker to cough and may make breathing more difficult, especially if the smoker has a cold or a breathing condition such as **asthma.**

Cigarette smoke irritates the throat and lungs.

Smoking and the body

Smoke is absorbed from the lungs into the bloodstream. The bloodstream carries nicotine to every organ in the body. Chewing tobacco is absorbed into the bloodstream through tissues in the mouth.

When a cigarette is burned, it produces a poisonous gas called **carbon monoxide.** Smokers inhale the carbon monoxide, and the gas takes the place of some of the **oxygen** in the blood. All the organs and tissues in the body need oxygen to function properly. People who have a lot of carbon monoxide in their bodies from smoking may tire more easily than nonsmokers when exercising. Heavy smokers may even experience vision problems or get headaches from carbon monoxide.

Smoking also causes **blood vessels** to **constrict** (get narrower), forcing the heart to work harder and **blood pressure** to rise. A smoker's heart rate may increase up to 30 percent while he or she is smoking.

Case Study

Kevin played on his school's baseball team. He was in top physical shape and could run a mile (1.6 kilometers) in six minutes. Then he started smoking one pack of cigarettes a day. Soon he found it took eight minutes to run the same distance, and the running made him wheeze.

Trachea

Bronchus

Alveoli

Bronchiole

Cigarette smoke goes directly to the lungs, where it is absorbed into the bloodstream and carried to every organ in the body.

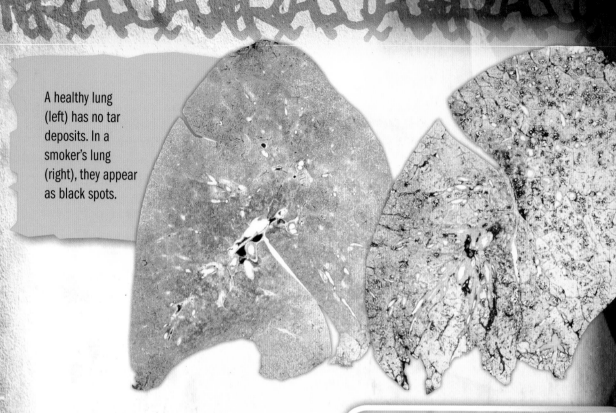
A healthy lung (left) has no tar deposits. In a smoker's lung (right), they appear as black spots.

Long-term effects

Tobacco smoke contains more than 4,800 chemicals, 69 of which are known to cause cancer. Some of these chemicals include:

- arsenic, an ingredient in rat poison
- ammonia, a substance used in cleaning products
- turpentine, a substance used for stripping paint
- butane, a component of gasoline
- formaldehyde, a substance used to preserve dead bodies

Cigarette smoke also contains tiny particles of **tar** that harden into a brown sticky substance in the lungs. Tar buildup in the lungs keeps them from functioning properly. It can lead to serious illnesses such as lung cancer and **emphysema**.

NEWSFLASH

Many smokers use cigarettes labeled "light" or "low tar" or smoke filtered cigarettes. They believe these cigarettes have less nicotine and tar. Recent research has shown that these smokers are just as likely to get lung cancer and other smoking-related illnesses as other smokers. This may be because they inhale more deeply when they smoke these cigarettes.

Smoker's cough

Inhaling smoke makes smokers produce excess **phlegm**, causing them to cough. Many smokers develop a cough that never seems to go away completely, even when they are not smoking. Smokers also get sick more often than nonsmokers—not just from diseases related to smoking, but also from other illnesses such as colds and flu. This is because smoking makes their **immune systems** work less efficiently.

Smoking and appearance

Smoking changes the way a person looks. Tobacco can leave yellow stains on a person's teeth and fingernails. It can also damage gums and cause bad breath. In addition, smoking damages tiny blood vessels in the skin. Because the blood vessels are damaged, the skin does not get the oxygen and other nutrients it needs. This causes the smoker's skin to age faster.

Smokers cannot taste and smell things as well as nonsmokers can. Over time, smoking deadens a person's sense of taste and smell.

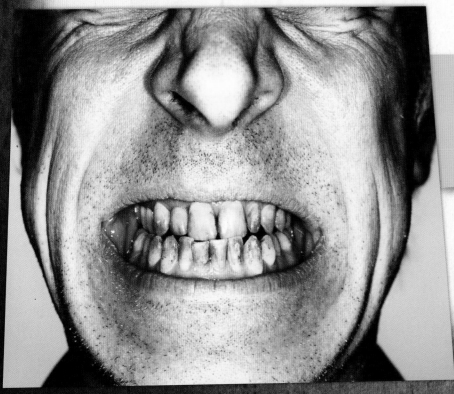

Tobacco stains teeth and damages gums.

Life-threatening illnesses

Smoking can do serious damage to the body. Smokers put themselves at risk for a variety of illnesses and even death. Each year, more than 400,000 people die prematurely from smoking-related illnesses in the United States. One in five deaths in the United States is linked to smoking. That makes smoking the number one cause of preventable deaths in the country.

Many of the chemicals in tobacco can cause cancer. The most common kind of cancer caused by smoking is lung cancer. Tobacco also causes cancers of the mouth, throat, stomach, kidney, **pancreas**, and **bladder**, as well as some kinds of **leukemia**.

Smoking damages the tiny airways in the lungs and causes the lungs to become inflamed. Damaged and inflamed lungs can cause long-term and even permanent lung diseases, including emphysema, **bronchitis**, and asthma.

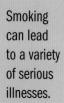

Smoking can lead to a variety of serious illnesses.

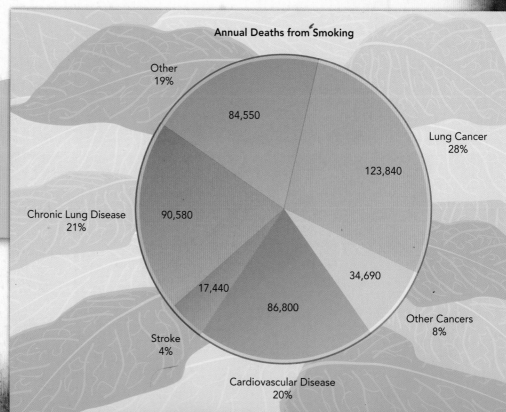

Annual Deaths from Smoking

Other
19%
84,550

Lung Cancer
28%
123,840

Chronic Lung Disease
21%
90,580

Other Cancers
8%
34,690

17,440

86,800

Stroke
4%

Cardiovascular Disease
20%

Some chemicals in tobacco products also damage the heart and blood vessels. These chemicals can cause a substance called **plaque** to build up inside the blood vessels. Plaque buildup decreases the amount of blood that can flow through blood vessels, sometimes resulting in blood clots. Blood clots can lead to strokes and heart attacks. Smokers are twice as likely to die of a heart attack as nonsmokers are.

Smoking during pregnancy

Smoking can harm babies that are still in the womb. When a pregnant woman smokes, her smoking affects her unborn baby. Babies of mothers who smoke are more likely to be born dead than those of nonsmokers. Babies of smoking mothers are also at risk for being born too small and for having poorly developed lungs.

Case Study

Gruen Von Behren started using chewing tobacco when he was 13 years old. At 17, he was diagnosed with cancer of the mouth. After many painful treatments and 40 surgeries, Gruen is still alive, but his face is severely disfigured. Gruen gives speeches at high schools encouraging teens not to use tobacco products.

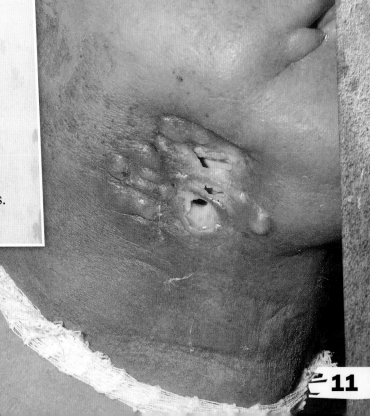

Tobacco products can cause disfiguring cancers, especially in the mouth and throat.

Social Effects

Smoking affects the way a person lives his or her life. Most smokers find it difficult to go more than a few hours without a cigarette. Many smokers have their first cigarette of the day within 15 minutes of waking up. A smoker who smokes a pack a day must find time to smoke 20 cigarettes throughout the day. Some smokers smoke two or even three packs every day.

Smoking bans

Finding a place to smoke has become more difficult in recent years. Most states in the U.S. have banned smoking in workplaces, at restaurants, and in other public areas. Smoking is also banned on airplanes, trains, and buses, making long trips difficult for smokers.

In many places, smoking is looked down upon, and smokers may be treated unfavorably. Some religions, such as Mormonism, do not permit their members to smoke. Many nonsmokers do not want smokers to smoke in their homes or cars. Landlords may refuse to rent property to smokers. In some states, employers can refuse to hire someone because he or she smokes.

People are no longer allowed to smoke in many public places.

Smoking bans force people who want to smoke at work to go outdoors to do it.

Teenage smokers

Teenagers who smoke may have more trouble in school than their nonsmoking classmates. Smokers often get poor grades and are more likely to get suspended from school than nonsmokers are. In addition, teenagers who smoke are more likely to use drugs and alcohol than those who do not smoke.

Smoking is expensive. A pack of cigarettes costs about $5. That means that a pack-a-day smoker will spend about $150 each month on cigarettes—more than $1,800 each year!

Case Study

Jenna started smoking when she was 14. She got her cigarettes from friends and then started buying them at a store where they did not ask for identification. When the store started checking identification, Jenna waited outside the door and asked strangers to buy cigarettes for her.

Spending time in smoky places can be dangerous, even for nonsmokers.

Secondhand smoke

Smoking affects more than just the smoker. A smoker inhales only a small amount of the smoke from a cigarette. The rest of the smoke pollutes the air. This polluted air is called secondhand smoke. People who are near a smoker end up breathing the secondhand smoke. By breathing in secondhand smoke, even nonsmokers can experience some of the negative effects of smoking.

Adult nonsmokers who frequently breathe in secondhand smoke increase their risk for lung cancer and heart disease by 25 to 30 percent. People who work at restaurants and bars in states without smoking bans breathe in a great deal of secondhand smoke. Family members of smokers are also often exposed to large amounts of secondhand smoke. Many nonsmokers have gotten sick and even died because their spouses were smokers.

What do you think?

Many smokers believe they have the right to smoke wherever they want and that smoking bans limit their rights. Most nonsmokers do not think they should have to breathe polluted air. Do you think smokers should be able to smoke wherever they want?

Secondhand smoke and children

Children are the greatest victims of secondhand smoke. Nearly 25 percent of children in the United States live in homes with at least one smoking adult. When parents or older siblings smoke around children, they are putting them at risk for asthma, ear infections, **pneumonia**, and bronchitis, as well as slowed lung growth. Smokers who live with nonsmokers can help to keep their loved ones safe by smoking in another room or outdoors.

Young children are often forced to breathe their parents' secondhand smoke.

Who Uses Tobacco?

The first people to use tobacco were the native people of North America and South America. In some tribes, tobacco was smoked only in ceremonies and was used by leaders and healers. In other tribes, tobacco use was more widespread. Christopher Columbus and other explorers brought tobacco back to Europe. Tobacco soon became a profitable crop for American colonists, who sold it in Europe and Asia. Today tobacco products can be found in almost every corner of the world.

At first no one knew that tobacco was harmful. Many people even thought it was healthy and could cure illnesses. More and more people began to smoke. During wartime, smoking increased even more. Soldiers received cigarettes along with food and other necessities in both World War I and World War II. Many young men entered the army as nonsmokers and came out addicted to cigarettes.

In the 1950s, most people did not know that smoking was dangerous.

Tobacco's peak

Smoking reached its peak in the 1960s, when the health risks of smoking became more well known. In 1964, the **surgeon general** released a study showing that tobacco caused serious health problems. Most people were surprised to learn that smoking was dangerous. Many people quit immediately. In 1966, tobacco companies were required to put the surgeon general's warning on their products, so that everyone would know that using tobacco is dangerous. Since then, the percentage of smokers in the United States has decreased steadily.

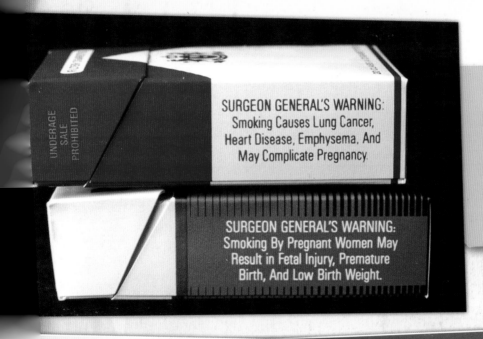

Since 1966, warnings such as these have appeared on all tobacco products.

What do you think?

For many years, tobacco companies sold their products without telling the public about the dangers of smoking. Now people who have suffered serious illnesses or lost loved ones from smoking may **sue** tobacco companies. The tobacco companies say that people make their own choices and that they have never forced anyone to smoke. Do you think tobacco companies should have to pay?

Who smokes today?

Forty-four million adults smoke in the United States. That is about one of every five people. Slightly more men smoke than women. People who have less money are more likely to smoke. Almost a third of the people who live below the poverty line use tobacco products. Poor people may be more likely to start smoking because they feel that even though smoking is expensive, it is one of the few pleasures they can afford. Once addicted, poor smokers may have a harder time quitting because they cannot afford therapies that might help them to give up cigarettes.

Education also plays a role. The more educated people are about the dangers of smoking, the less likely they are to smoke. In general, the less education a person has, the more likely he or she is to smoke.

It is illegal for people under the age of 18 to buy tobacco products.

NEWSFLASH

A study completed in 2003 found that over half of underage smokers buy their cigarettes either by purchasing them themselves or by paying another person to buy them. Young smokers also "bum" cigarettes from other people. About one in ten teenage smokers has stolen cigarettes from another person or from a store.

One in five high
school seniors uses
tobacco regularly.

Teenagers and children

Even though it is illegal for people under 18 years old to buy or
use tobacco products in the United States, a higher percentage of
teenagers smoke than adults. Twenty-three percent of high school
students in the United States are regular smokers. Some younger
teens also smoke, although it is less common. Eight percent of
middle school students are regular smokers.

Some young people prefer *bidis* and *kreteks* to cigarettes. About
three percent of high school students smoke *bidis* or *kreteks*. Many
young people believe that *bidis* and *kreteks* are less dangerous than
cigarettes, but this is not true. *Bidis* and *kreteks* have higher levels of
nicotine, tar, and carbon monoxide than cigarettes do.

Why People Smoke

No one plans to get addicted to cigarettes when they take their first puff, but that is exactly what happens to many young people. Every day nearly 4,000 people aged 12 to 17 years old try smoking for the first time. Of these, more than 1,000 will become daily smokers. Ninety percent of adult smokers started smoking before the age of 21.

For many people, smoking begins at home. Teenagers who live in homes where parents or siblings smoke are four times more likely to become smokers than those who live with nonsmokers.

Teenagers often get cigarettes from their friends.

Case Study

Leah started smoking when she was just nine years old. She wanted to fit in with older kids who smoked. Most of Leah's family members are smokers, and some of them have died from cancer. Leah is worried about her own smoking and wants to quit.

Many teenagers start smoking because they think it will help them make friends.

Peer pressure

Many teenagers start smoking because of **peer pressure.** Peer pressure is when one person makes another person feel that he or she must act or look a certain way in order to fit in. Teenagers often think that they will be rejected by a group or be made fun of if they do not smoke. Many teenagers find themselves addicted to cigarettes because they were afraid to say no.

Teenagers do not have to be afraid to say no. Most young people do not smoke. They will support their peers' decision not to smoke, too. Parents, counselors, and teachers can also offer help and support for staying away from tobacco. Teenagers who are feeling the effects of peer pressure should talk to an adult that they like and trust. In addition, teenagers should remember that there are much better ways to fit into a group than by smoking. Joining an after-school club or sports team is a fun and healthy way to make friends.

Even though tobacco companies are banned from advertising on TV, they can still sponsor sporting events.

Tobacco's targets

Tobacco companies know that most of their customers start smoking when they are young, so they create advertising that appeals to teenagers and children. In the late 1980s, one tobacco company used a cartoon camel to promote its products. "Joe Camel" became as well known as Mickey Mouse, and cigarette sales skyrocketed.

In 1998, tobacco companies were forbidden to market their products to children, and cartoon characters were banned from tobacco advertisements. It is now illegal for cigarette companies to advertise on TV, radio, billboards, or the Internet in the United States. However, tobacco companies can still advertise in magazines, and can sponsor sports, entertainment, and other events.

NEWSFLASH

In the past, one way that cigarette companies appealed to teenagers was to sell candy- and fruit-flavored cigarettes. But that will not happen anymore. In October 2006, as part of a lawsuit settlement with 37 states, tobacco companies agreed to take the flavored cigarettes off the market.

Antismoking campaigns

Antismoking groups have fought back against the tobacco companies by launching several successful advertising campaigns. Their ads encourage young people not to smoke. The MTV "Truth" ads have had a powerful impact on young people. These ads make the effects of smoking graphically clear, and are credited with a decrease in teenage smoking.

The attorneys general of 41 states have come up with a new use for the "Truth" ads. In September 2006, they wrote a letter asking movie studios to include a "Truth" ad on DVDs of movies that feature people smoking. Research has shown that teenagers are strongly influenced when they see celebrities smoking in movies. The "Truth" ads on the DVDs would let teens know that although smoking might look appealing in the movies, in reality it can lead to horrible diseases and death.

Antismoking ads are an effective way to teach teens about the dangers of smoking.

No More Nicotine

Most smokers know that tobacco is bad for them and want to quit. Seventy percent of teenage smokers say they wish that they had never started smoking. However, nicotine is extremely addictive, and quitting is difficult. Every year, 40 percent of smokers try to quit, but only five percent succeed on their first try. These numbers look discouraging, but even smokers who fail should not give up. Most smokers try and fail several times before finally stopping for good.

Quitting is difficult because **withdrawal** symptoms and the cravings for a cigarette are usually very intense. Withdrawal symptoms occur because a smoker's body is physically dependent on nicotine. When the body is deprived of nicotine, a smoker can experience a wide variety of symptoms, including:

- depression
- irritability
- trouble sleeping
- trouble concentrating
- restlessness
- headache
- upset stomach
- tiredness
- increased appetite

Quitting smoking is difficult, but it can be done.

The most severe withdrawal symptoms usually disappear within a few days. The rest of the symptoms and cravings fade over a period of weeks, although smokers can experience cravings years after they smoked their last cigarette.

People who quit smoking feel healthier and can perform better athletically.

Top Tips

The March of Dimes gives these tips to teenagers who want to quit smoking:

- Write down why you want to stop smoking.
- Choose a "Quit Day" sometime in the next two weeks.
- Ask a nonsmoking friend or sibling to help you quit.
- Throw out all cigarettes, ashtrays, matches, and lighters on your "Quit Day."
- Stay away from places and activities that make you want to smoke.

Case Study

After three years of smoking, Pat quit when he was 19. He wanted to quit while he was still young so that his lungs would not be permanently damaged. Five months after quitting, he is thrilled that he can surf and play tennis better because his lungs are healthier.

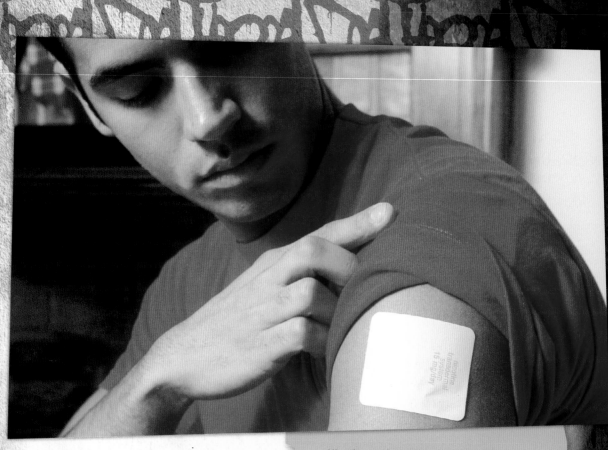

Nicotine replacement therapies like patches can help people to stop smoking.

Ways to quit

There are many ways to stop smoking, and different methods work for different people. Smokers often try to quit "cold turkey." This means giving up all forms of nicotine at once. It results in severe withdrawal symptoms, beginning within a few hours of smoking the last cigarette. Withdrawal symptoms make quitting cold turkey difficult, but if a smoker can make it through the first 72 hours, the worst of the symptoms disappear. Quitting cold turkey is the quickest way to get nicotine out of the body.

Top Tips

If your parents smoke at home, they are putting your health at risk as well as their own. Even if they want to quit, they may need encouragement to take the first step. Why not try asking them to quit? Make sure you explain why you would like them to quit, and try not to get angry. Let them know that their health is important to you. Quitting smoking is difficult, even for adults, so offer to help and support them as they try to quit.

Nicotine replacement therapy

Using nicotine replacement therapy is another way to quit smoking. Instead of smoking, the person uses a nicotine replacer such as a nicotine patch, nasal spray, or chewing gum. These give the user a limited amount of nicotine. Over a period of weeks or months, the amount is gradually reduced until the user is no longer addicted to nicotine.

Some people find that using the nonnicotine drugs **bupropion** and **varenicline** can reduce withdrawal symptoms. These drugs must be prescribed by a doctor and can be used along with other methods.

Most people who quit say that support from family and friends is important. Many people also benefit from individual or group counseling. Most states also offer phone "hotlines" that people can call for advice and support. The hotlines are free and available 24 hours a day.

Tobacco hotlines offer support for people who are trying to quit smoking.

Saying No to Tobacco

Even though you know that using tobacco products is dangerous and addictive, it may still be hard to say no when a friend offers you a cigarette. Here are some tips for dealing with peer pressure.

First, remember:

- You do not have to do anything that you do not want to do.

- It is perfectly okay to say no. You do not owe anyone an explanation.

- Most young people do not smoke, so you are in good company.

It is a good idea to have an answer ready for someone who offers you a cigarette. Try to find a reason to say no that is true for you.

- If you are allergic to smoke or if you do not like the smell, you can use that as a reason for not smoking.

- If you will get in trouble from your parents or from a coach for smoking, you can give that as a reason.

- If your parents or others you know smoke, you can talk about how you would like them to quit, so you do not smoke yourself.

- You can always say that smoking can kill you and cause serious diseases such as cancer.

Real friends will respect your decision. If someone will not stop pressuring you to smoke, it is okay to ask for help from an adult you trust, such as a teacher or counselor.

Tobacco Facts

- Forty-four million adults smoke in the United States. That is just over 20 percent of the population, or one in every five people.

- Ninety percent of adult smokers started smoking before the age of 21.

- Every day, nearly 4,000 people aged 12 to 17 years old try smoking for the first time. Of these, more than 1,000 become daily smokers.

- Twenty-three percent of high-school students in the United States are regular smokers.

- Eight percent of middle-school students are regular smokers.

- Ten percent of male high-school students use smokeless tobacco such as chew and snuff regularly.

- Four percent of male middle-school students use smokeless tobacco regularly.

- Each year, more than 400,000 people in the United States die prematurely from using tobacco products.

- One in every five deaths in the United States is related to smoking.

- Nearly 25 percent of children in the United States live in homes with at least one smoking adult.

- Adult nonsmokers who frequently breathe secondhand smoke increase their risk for lung cancer and cardiac disease by 25 to 30 percent.

- Smokers are more likely than nonsmokers to use drugs and alcohol.

- Tobacco companies spend more than $15 billion per year on advertising and promotion. That is more than $40 million every day.

- A smoker who smokes a pack of cigarettes a day spends more than $1,800 each year on cigarettes. Many smokers smoke more than a pack a day.

Glossary

addictive causing the body to become dependent

asthma usually chronic lung condition that causes coughing, wheezing, and breathing problems

bladder baglike organ where urine is stored before it leaves the body

blood pressure pressure of the blood against the walls of the blood vessels

blood vessel tube in the body that carries blood to tissues and organs

bronchitis disease caused by the swelling of the bronchial tubes in the lungs

bupropion prescription drug used to treat depression or to help a person quit smoking tobacco

carbon monoxide poisonous gas

cocaine illegal and highly addictive drug derived from the coca plant

constrict to make narrower

craving extremely strong desire

emphysema serious disease in which the air sacs in the lungs become enlarged and damaged, making breathing difficult

heroin illegal and highly addictive drug derived from the pain reliever morphine

immune system body's system for protecting itself from illness and disease

leukemia often fatal form of cancer in which the body produces too many white blood cells

nicotine poisonous and addictive substance found in the tobacco plant

oxygen gas that is essential for life

pancreas large gland behind the stomach that helps the body digest food

peer pressure social pressure to behave or look a certain way in order to be accepted by a group

phlegm thick mucus secreted by the respiratory system

plaque deposits of fatty material that build up on the inner walls of blood vessels

pneumonia illness in which the lungs become inflamed

sue take legal action against someone

surgeon general head of public health services at the state or federal level

tar dark, sticky residue from tobacco smoke

varenicline prescription drug that can reduce the withdrawal symptoms when a person stops smoking tobacco

withdrawal unpleasant physical and emotional symptoms that occur when a person gives up a substance on which he or she was dependent

Further Resources

Books

Gleason, Carrie. *The Biography of Tobacco.* New York: Crabtree Publishing Company, 2006.

Green, Carl R. *Nicotine and Tobacco.* Berkeley Heights, N.J.: Enslow Publishers Inc., 2005.

Landau, Elaine. *Cigarettes.* New York: Franklin Watts, 2003.

Sanders, Bruce. *Let's Talk About Smoking.* Mankato, Minn.: Stargazer Books, 2005.

Websites

CDC Tips4Youth
www.cdc.gov/tobacco/tips4youth.htm

CHAMPSS (Children Helping and Motivating Parents to Stop Smoking)
www.champss.org/

COST (Children Opposed to Smoking Tobacco)
www.costkids.org

Organizations

Action on Smoking and Health (ASH)
2013 H St. NW
Washington DC, 20006
Website: www.ash.org

American Cancer Society (ACS)
1599 Clifton Rd. NE
Atlanta, GA 30329
Website: www.cancer.org

American Lung Association (ALA)
61 Broadway, 6th Floor
New York, NY 10006
Website: www.lungusa.org

Index